EGMONT

We bring stories to life

First published in Great Britain 2017 by Egmont UK Limited
The Yellow Building, 1 Nicholas Road
London W11 4AN

Written by Stephanie Milton.
Additional material by Max Brooks, Joseph Garrett, Sarah Brown, Lizzie Dwyer, Marsh Davies, Ninni Landin, Michael Stoyke, Jens Bergensten, Daniel Wustenhoff, Agnes Larsson, Leonard Gram, Patrick Geuder and Mariana Graham.
Designed by Paul Lang and John Stuckey.
Illustrations by Ryan Marsh.
Cover illustration by Ryan Marsh.
Production by Stef Fischetti and Laura Grundy.
MINECON photos © Mojang AB.
Special thanks to Lydia Winters, Owen Jones, Junkboy, Martin Johansson and Marsh Davies.

Shutterstock.com image credits: Jaromir Grich, InnaVar, SHTRAUS DMYTRO, David Hughes, Zita, Volodymyr Goinyk, SusaZoom, kostasgr, Victor Moussa, okeykat, artshock, Christopher Elwell, Budkov Denis, Cantemir Olaru, TeodorLazarev, Africa Studio, Creative Travel Projects, junglefiend, AnatSkwong, Fokin Oleg, MarcelClemens, VallaV, Max Sudakov, Catalin Petolea, Madlen, Saurav022, Noofoo Media Limited, Authentic travel.

MOJANG

ISBN 978 1 4052 8758 6

66813/7
Printed in EU

Parental guidance is advised for all outdoor activities.

ONLINE SAFETY FOR YOUNGER FANS
Spending time online is great fun! Here are a few simple rules to help younger fans stay safe and keep the internet a great place to spend time:

- Never give out your real name – don't use it as your username.
- Never give out any of your personal details.
- Never tell anybody which school you go to or how old you are.
- Never tell anybody your password except a parent or a guardian.
- Be aware that you must be 13 or over to create an account on many sites.
Always check the site policy and ask a parent or guardian for permission before registering.
- Always tell a parent or guardian if something is worrying you.

Stay safe online. Any website addresses listed in this book are correct at the time of going to print. However, Egmont is not responsible for content hosted by third parties. Please be aware that online content can be subject to change and websites can contain content that is unsuitable for children.
We advise that all children are supervised when using the internet.

ANNUAL 2018

CONTENTS

4

HELLO!

Welcome to the Minecraft Annual 2018! Thanks for joining us as we take a look back across the last 12 months of Minecraft fun!

It's been a truly thrilling year for us – which is fitting given that 2017 was officially the Year of Adventure! (Officially decided by us, anyway!) We've had some major updates, making the game bigger, better and more beautiful than ever before. Terracotta and coloured clays put an even prettier palette in the hands of players, and the entire game got a nice coat of gloss with the Super Fancy Graphics Pack. We made it easier for players to get together, regardless of what kind of shiny computing device you play on, and we created new ways to explore the amazing stuff made by the rest of our awesome, ingenious community. Oh, and we added parrots. Pretty cool.

Outside of the game, we were pretty busy, too. We rejigged how MINECON works, so an even larger number of you could join in the fun, put Minecraft: Education Edition in classrooms the world over, and, through our Block by Block charity, continued to help ordinary people redesign the public spaces in which they live – using Minecraft!

Above all, we've been inspired by the amazing stuff that you, the players, have been up to. The things you've built, the challenges you've set yourself, the stories you've told – it's an honour for us to be a part of that! In these pages you can see some of the ambitious builds, adventures and experiences the community made, along with loads of ideas for your own projects, tips, tricks and a few contributions from famous friends!

Dig in and enjoy!

Marsh Davies,
Mojang

THE ADVENTURER'S INVENTORY

In Minecraft's Year of Adventure you'll no doubt feel inspired to embark on an epic Survival adventure of your own. Here's a rundown of the key items and companions you'll need to take with you on your journey.

4 SHIELD
A shield will help you block incoming attacks. They're easy to make, and you can customise them with your favourite banners and enchant them to make them more effective.

1 ENCHANTED DIAMOND SWORD
The ultimate melee weapon, an enchanted diamond sword will deal maximum damage in hand-to-hand combat. Hostile mobs will be running in fear!

2 ENCHANTED DIAMOND ARMOUR
Enchanted diamond armour will keep you safer than any other armour. If you don't have quite enough diamond, then enchanted iron armour is the next best alternative.

3 TAMED WOLVES
Tamed wolves will attack any mob that injures you, and will attack skeletons without provocation. You'll need to tame them with bones to earn their loyalty.

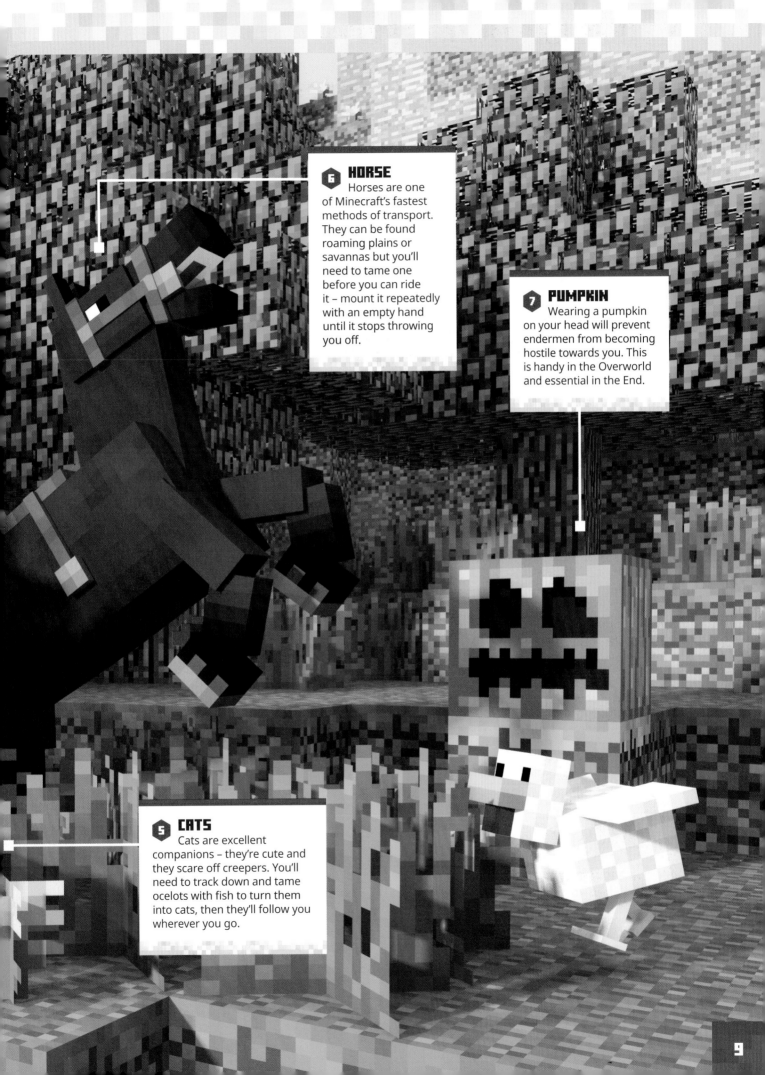

HORSE

6 Horses are one of Minecraft's fastest methods of transport. They can be found roaming plains or savannas but you'll need to tame one before you can ride it – mount it repeatedly with an empty hand until it stops throwing you off.

PUMPKIN

7 Wearing a pumpkin on your head will prevent endermen from becoming hostile towards you. This is handy in the Overworld and essential in the End.

CATS

5 Cats are excellent companions – they're cute and they scare off creepers. You'll need to track down and tame ocelots with fish to turn them into cats, then they'll follow you wherever you go.

THE ADVENTURER'S INVENTORY

GOLDEN APPLES

Golden apples help you heal by providing regeneration II and absorption I. They can be crafted with gold ingots and found in some chests.

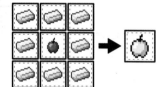

GOLDEN APPLE RECIPE

FLINT AND STEEL

A flint and steel creates fire. You'll need it to light TNT and activate Nether portals. It's crafted from an iron ingot and flint.

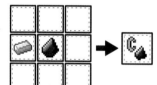

FLINT AND STEEL RECIPE

BED

Beds let you sleep through the night and avoid the hostile mobs that come out when it gets dark. You'll need wood planks and wool.

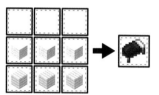

BED RECIPE

TNT

TNT allows you to blow up multiple enemies and large areas of land. It's crafted from sand and gunpowder.

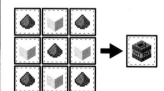

TNT RECIPE

COMPASS

This handy tool points to your spawn point. You'll need redstone and iron ingots to craft one.

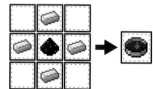

COMPASS RECIPE

BOAT

A boat allows you to travel across large expanses of water more quickly and is crafted from wood planks.

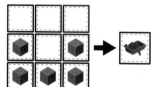

BOAT RECIPE

POTIONS

Potions of Healing, Regeneration, Strength and Fire Resistance are always handy. You'll need a brewing stand to make potions. It's crafted from cobblestone and a blaze rod and fueled with blaze powder.

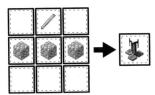

BREWING STAND RECIPE

You'll need to make awkward potion first, by brewing a water bottle with Nether wart.

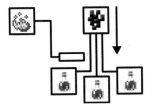

Brew your awkward potion with glistering melon, a ghast tear, blaze powder or magma cream to get the desired potion. Most of these ingredients can be found in the Nether.

POTION OF HEALING RECIPE

POTION OF REGENERATION RECIPE

POTION OF STRENGTH RECIPE

POTION OF FIRE RESISTANCE RECIPE

SPLASH POTIONS

These throwable potions come in handy as weapons. They are brewed by adding gunpowder to a regular potion on a brewing stand.

Brew a water bottle with a fermented spider eye to make potion of weakness, then brew this potion with gunpowder to turn it into a splash potion. Fermented spider eye is crafted from a spider eye, a brown mushroom and sugar.

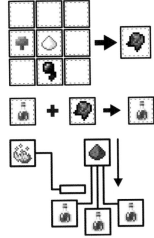

SPLASH POTION OF WEAKNESS

Brew awkward potion with a spider eye to make potion of poison, then brew this with gunpowder to turn it into a splash potion.

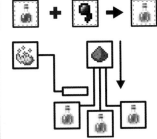

SPLASH POTION OF POISON

SADDLE

You'll need a saddle to ride a horse, and horses are one of the fastest ways to travel long distances. Saddles can be found in naturally generated chests.

ENDER PEARLS

Ender pearls will come in handy when you're ready to find a stronghold and visit the End. They're dropped by endermen when they die and can be found in some naturally generated chests.

FOOD

You'll need plenty of food to keep your strength up. High quality food like steak and cooked pork chops are ideal as they restore 8 food points.

MOJANG'S MEMORABLE ADVENTURING MOMENTS

Whether it's playing Hardcore Survival mode or building ingenious creations, the Mojang team have had their fair share of adventures. Check out their most memorable adventuring moments!

I'm mostly into design, building villages and cities in particular. I have, however, taken notes on abandoned mine locations I've stumbled across by accident. When I feel the urge to go on an adventure I simply visit one of those, set up a base camp and begin treasure hunting.

NINNI LANDIN
ARTIST

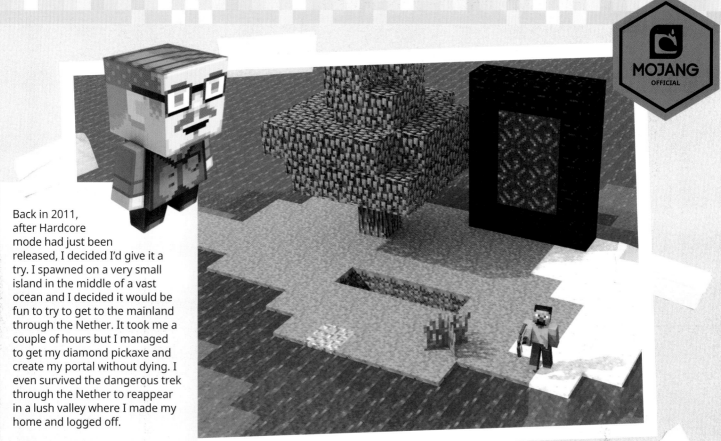

Back in 2011, after Hardcore mode had just been released, I decided I'd give it a try. I spawned on a very small island in the middle of a vast ocean and I decided it would be fun to try to get to the mainland through the Nether. It took me a couple of hours but I managed to get my diamond pickaxe and create my portal without dying. I even survived the dangerous trek through the Nether to reappear in a lush valley where I made my home and logged off.

LEONARD GRAM
DEVELOPER

I had just joined Mojang and my young nephews were spending the summer with us. The older one, who was 8, had recently discovered Minecraft. The younger one, who was 6, was new to the game and cheered me on as I ventured out in a new Survival world. Being flanked by a Minecraft pro and an adventurous youngster was great. One provided every imaginable recipe, and the other a constant commentary on every discovery. During our first adventure my oldest nephew pointed out that I was hungry and that there was a pig close by. The younger one directed me on how to sneak up on the pig, and I killed it for chops. My younger, now noticeably shaken, nephew told me in a faint voice, 'It's OK to kill pigs in Minecraft. They're not real.'

PATRICK GEUDER
DIRECTOR OF BUSINESS DEVELOPMENT

My Realm buddies and I have spent many nights trying to make a minecart-chest storage system, where, at the push of a button, a chest would be delivered to your location so you can get your blocks and items delivered to the central city bank. We spent many late nights debugging the redstone signals and rail switches, but it was a lot of fun standing spread across the map, waiting for minecarts to show up.

DANIEL WUSTENHOFF
DEVELOPER

My server is all about role-playing and storytelling. I love to go out on adventures to see what will happen, what we'll explore and to see how it can contribute to the story of the world! Once, after a few in-game days of horseback riding we came to a beautiful savanna, and soon after we also found a charming village. We decided that the village was the main settlement in an ancient, but still active, savanna kingdom called Sendario. The village was called Sendira. 'Sendario' and 'Sendira' are words developed from the language spoken by the people of the great savanna kingdom.

AGNES LARSSON
DEVELOPER

Back when the game was still in beta I was live streaming to show off new features such as the eye of ender. I felt short on time, so I rushed to get to the Nether and find blaze powder as quickly as possible. That turned into a situation where I was exploring the Nether fortress without any armour and only equipped with a stone sword. I got into a battle with a blaze, and by sheer luck I managed to defeat it and escape with a half heart of health remaining. That was really scary and lots of people were watching!

JENS BERGENSTEN
DEVELOPER

I've been browsing old backups from around two years ago, trying to sort them out. In one of the old backups I found something that I thought was lost forever – the very first world I ever played in Minecraft. It was in version Alpha 1.1.2_02 and I had to use that old version to open the world without conversion artifacts. So I installed the old version of Minecraft and copied the world save from my backup, and found everything that I built before, just as I remember it. It was amazing and I spent every evening for over a week playing the old version again and enjoying the world that was my introduction to the game. Usually I play with music turned off, but in this old world I had to turn the music back on for maximum nostalgia.

MICHAEL STOYKE
DEVELOPER

ADVENTURE MODE

Did you know there's an entire mode in Minecraft called Adventure mode? It's a game mode that allows you to create epic adventure maps. If you're serious about creating an adventure map, this is the mode for you.

SO WHAT ARE THE BENEFITS OF ADVENTURE MODE?

In Adventure mode you can't break any useful blocks by hand. You can break them with the tool designed to break them, but only if that function has been allowed. You can use this function to stop griefers from destroying your constructions by ensuring they don't have the required tools to break the blocks, or the means to craft them. It also makes survival in general more difficult. You can't place any blocks in Adventure mode, either, which means you can't build anything new. You can still hit mobs, trade with NPC villagers and use furnaces. You can choose to add bonus chests to help players out. These chests are filled with basic items that will help players survive.

DID YOU KNOW?

This ancient temple is part of an adventure map called 'The Forgotten Book' by Foleros, Tomaxed and L4PS.

HOW DO YOU USE ADVENTURE MODE?

You can switch to Adventure mode from any other mode by typing one of the following when in a game:

`/gamemode 2`

`/gamemode adventure`

DID YOU KNOW?

Adventure mode was originally called Dungeons and Levers.

WHAT TO DO NEXT

You might choose to play alone in Adventure mode, instead of Survival mode, to give yourself more of a challenge. Or you might build an amazing adventure map for other players to try. There are some amazing examples of Adventure mode maps on the next few pages, which take advantage of the mode's features.

REALMS

The bravest Minecraft adventurers can test their skills on Realms, where Mojang has carefully curated worlds, adventure maps and experiences for everyone to enjoy. Let's take a look at some of the Realms content from the past year to give you a taste of what you can expect.

DID YOU KNOW?

Many Realms maps use custom texture packs to enhance the atmosphere. Luckily they're automatically downloaded when you enter the map. Handy!

BIG GIANT LIGHT SHOW

CDFMAN, SOUNAS AND SPIDERROBOTMAN

Big Giant Light Show is the first of Realms' new experiences, allowing you to experiment with exciting effects that haven't been part of the Realms experience to-date. You're in charge of the camera at a concert and it's your job to move around and take different shots of the show, which includes art builds, rollercoasters, fireworks and several BigGiantCircles tracks. The custom resource pack makes for a truly epic experience.

10 MINUTE PARKOUR

FANTOMLX, IWACKY AND TILIBA

This collection of 101 different maps will test your parkour skills to the limit. You have just ten minutes to complete as many of the mini arenas as possible, and you can play against the clock or against your friends. There are special blocks which will help or hinder you as you progress. You'll earn a point each time you complete a level, and you'll lose a point if you skip a level.

ELYTRON

THETICMAN AND CHILDOFSTARS

Did you know that elytron is the singular form of the word elytra, which is the two wing case of a beetle? As you know, elytra are wings in Minecraft that allow you to glide across the world, and they've been put to good use in this competitive minigame. The object of the game is to outlast your opponent by avoiding the glass trails as you soar across the arena using your elytra. You can team up with your friends or play against them and attempt to make them fly into the walls. Just remember to avoid your own walls.

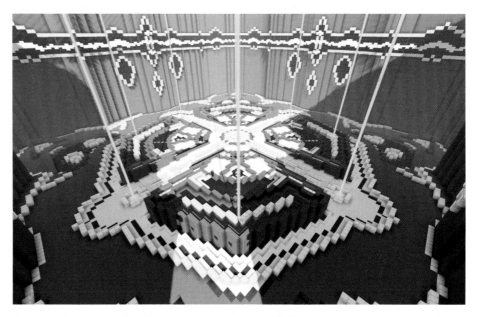

BATTLE OF GODS

MCMAKISTEIN, SQORED AND ENRAZEGAMES

In this dramatic minigame you'll become a God, gifted with special powers which you'll use to battle other players for possession of three valuable relics. You'll be able to blast people into the air or launch a ranged fireball attack as you attempt to grab the relics and return them to your home biome. There's also a single player mode so you can get to know the terrain and practise your skills before taking on other players.

THE FORGOTTEN BOOK

FOLEROS, TOMAXED AND L4PS

This adventure map takes you deep into a jungle where you'll find the ruins of an ancient civilisation. Your quest is to find a valuable magical book. Many have tried before you, and none have returned. As you explore you'll discover abandoned villages, temples and gemstones. Keep your wits about you and you could be the first to find the Forgotten Book.

ICE WARS

TEAM NOOT

Ice Wars is a fun player-versus-player (PVP) minigame in which you must battle your opponents across a dangerous expanse of water in an icy biome. In Deathmatch mode you'll race across the water using the frost walker enchantment to turn it into ice, and your goal is to knock your opponents into the dangerous water, causing them to freeze. In Destroy the Flag mode there are two camps and you must destroy the opposing team's flag before they destroy yours.

HIGHLINER

MCDIC AND KAYAN

If you like board games, you'll love Highliner. The object of this strategic, two-player game is to enclose your opponent's tiles with your own and change them to your colour. You can bridge spaces, make defensive moves and lock down tiles so that they can't be changed back to the other colour later. There are some awesome game mechanics at play, such as placed tiles falling from the sky and landing neatly on the board. This is a game you'll want to play more than once, as each time you play you'll learn some strategic new moves.

FROSTY WIND

THETICMAN AND CHILDOFSTARS

As any serious Minecraft explorer knows, ice spikes biomes are renowned for being cold, barren and inhospitable. But in this world template things are a little different, and someone's very kindly built a village that's all ready for you to move in and take shelter from the frosty winds. There are also some friendly snowman statues sitting among the ice spikes to make the place a little more welcoming. What you do once you've settled into your new home is up to you.

CHRISTMAS BRAWL

MINEMAKERS TEAM

Christmas Brawl is a PVP map with a festive twist and it's a great map to try during the winter holidays. The object is to eliminate all your opponents from the map. You can battle as all manner of creatures, from angry snowmen that can melt and teleport around the map, to furious reindeer with pointy antlers. If you want to win you'll have to defeat your friends and be the last player standing. There are power-ups to help you along the way.

THE NAUGHTY LIST

THE NAUGHTY ELVES

This festive minigame was a collaboration put together by a group of Realms contributors. You're one of Santa's elves, but you've crashed his sleigh and, as a punishment, he's put you on the Naughty List! In order to get back onto the Nice List you'll have to play games and build your Christmas Spirit. With any luck you'll be back on the Nice List just in time for Christmas.

WATER PARK BUILD CHALLENGE

Water rides are a fun alternative to rollercoasters and a popular build choice. This exciting water park will inspire you to create your own rides so you can invite your friends over to your world for a day of adventure.

2 LAZY RIVER RIDE
Build a lazy river ride around the entire water park. This ride is about relaxation, not thrills, so keep the twists and bumps to a minimum. Build a wide trough and provide boats for your guests to jump into. Make sure the ride gives the best views of the park and add some flowers and trees around the river ride.

1 BEACH
Swimming is hard work, so you'll need a relaxing beach area. Make sun loungers from quartz stairs and slabs. Parasols can be made from coloured blocks and fences. Coastal blues will really pop against the sandy backdrop and stripes are perfect for a beachy feel.

TIP

Try building your park in a desert biome to give it a summer feel.

3 BLACK HOLE
The black hole caters to the more daring among your guests. Players are dropped into a dark hole which swirls them around before dropping them into a splash pool below.

4 VIEWING PLATFORM
Create a viewing platform so guests can look out across the expanse of the water park. A lighthouse will work well with the aquatic theme and provides a high vantage point.

5 WATER FLUMES
Create water flumes from colourful blocks. They key is to add lots of twists and turns, and surprise drops and dark areas for maximum thrill-factor.

WATER PARK BUILD CHALLENGE

No beach area is complete without an ice cream truck. You can make one from quartz blocks and various colours of hardened clay. Place a jukebox on top and it can even play a tune to attract customers.

ICE CREAM TRUCK

🕐 15 MIN ❶ ⬡⬡⬡ EASY

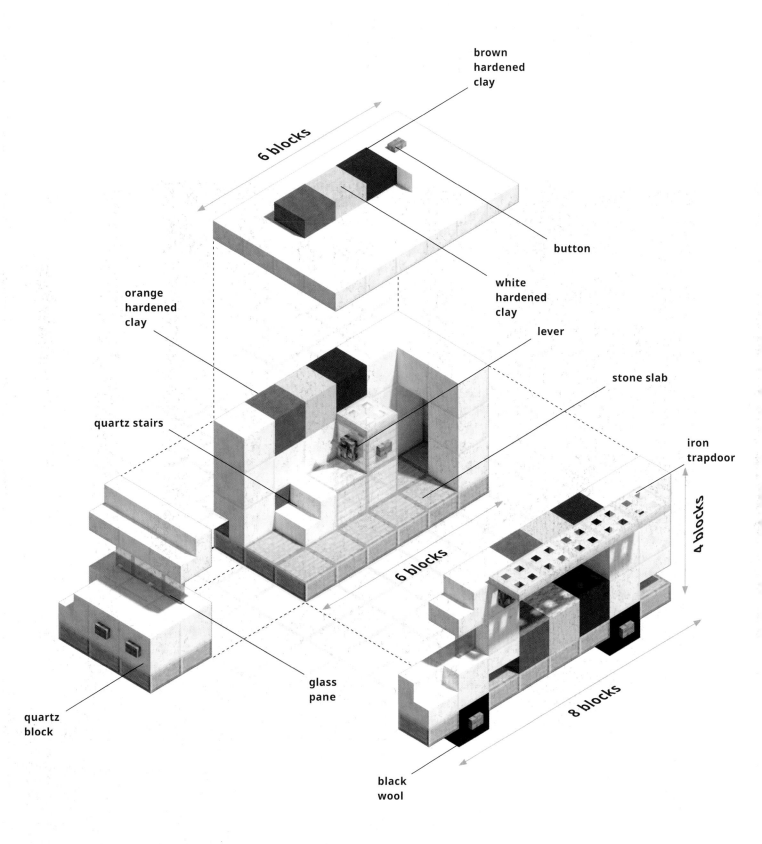

brown
hardened
clay

6 blocks

button

orange
hardened
clay

white
hardened
clay

lever

stone slab

quartz stairs

iron
trapdoor

4 blocks

6 blocks

glass
pane

quartz
block

8 blocks

black
wool

ABANDONED MINESHAFT SURVIVAL CHALLENGE

PART 1

Challenge yourself to restore an abandoned mineshaft so that it can be used for its intended purpose. These instructions will help you turn it into a working mine and eliminate any danger.

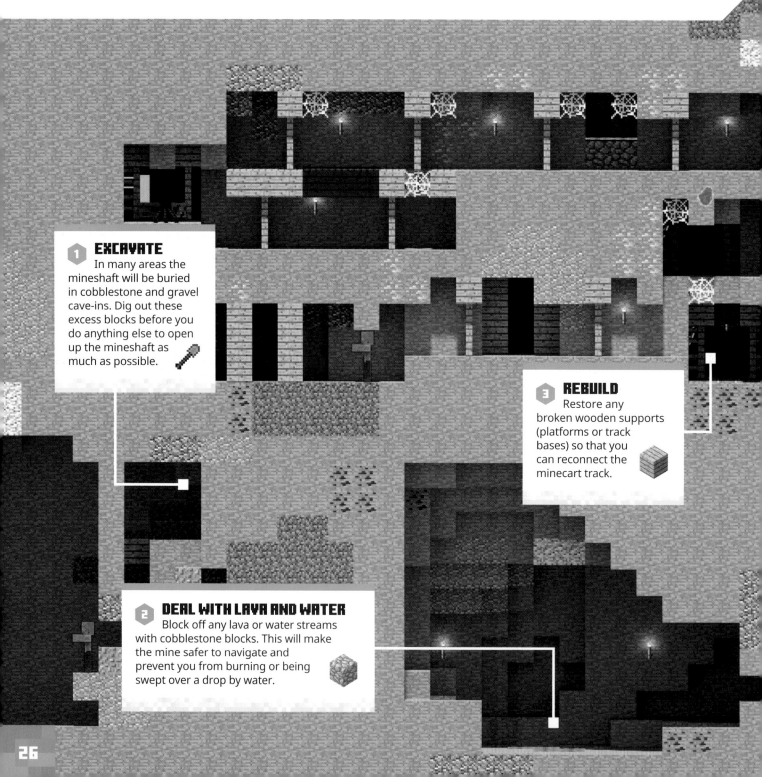

1 EXCAVATE
In many areas the mineshaft will be buried in cobblestone and gravel cave-ins. Dig out these excess blocks before you do anything else to open up the mineshaft as much as possible.

3 REBUILD
Restore any broken wooden supports (platforms or track bases) so that you can reconnect the minecart track.

2 DEAL WITH LAVA AND WATER
Block off any lava or water streams with cobblestone blocks. This will make the mine safer to navigate and prevent you from burning or being swept over a drop by water.

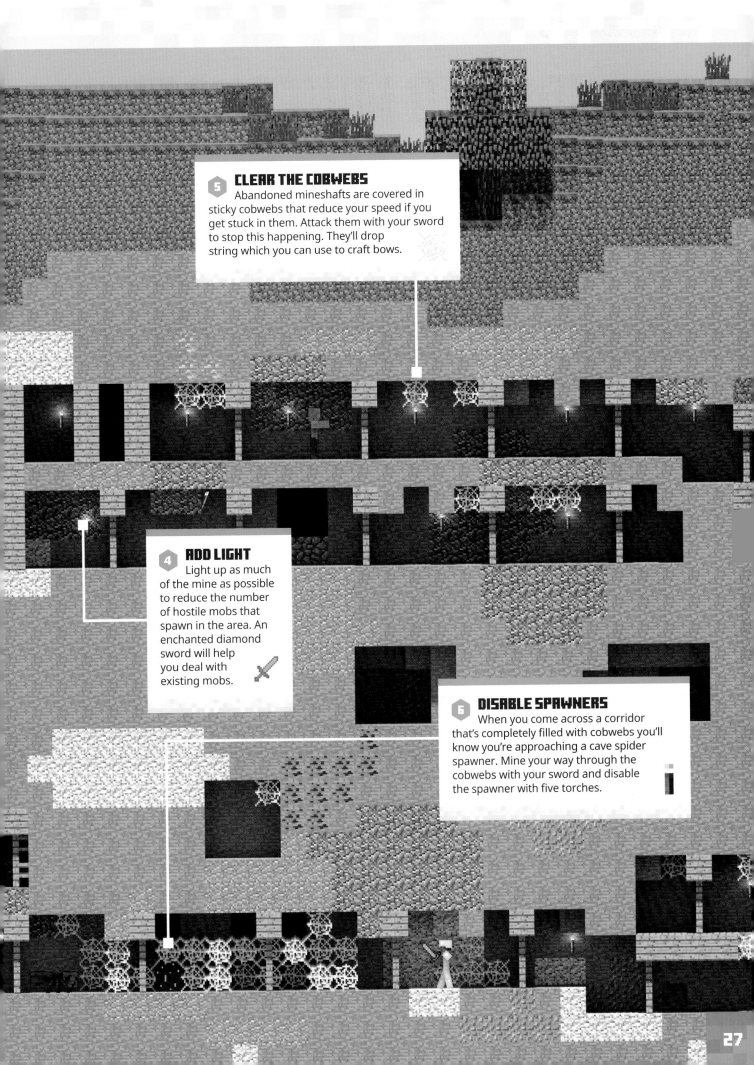

5 CLEAR THE COBWEBS

Abandoned mineshafts are covered in sticky cobwebs that reduce your speed if you get stuck in them. Attack them with your sword to stop this happening. They'll drop string which you can use to craft bows.

4 ADD LIGHT

Light up as much of the mine as possible to reduce the number of hostile mobs that spawn in the area. An enchanted diamond sword will help you deal with existing mobs.

6 DISABLE SPAWNERS

When you come across a corridor that's completely filled with cobwebs you'll know you're approaching a cave spider spawner. Mine your way through the cobwebs with your sword and disable the spawner with five torches.

ABANDONED MINESHAFT SURVIVAL CHALLENGE

PART 2 Now that the mineshaft is safer, you can build on the existing track structure and create a proper working minecart system with stations and junctions.

1 BUILD MINECART STATIONS

A minecart system needs minecart stations at strategic locations. Each station will need a dispenser full of minecarts.

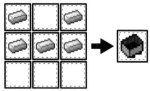

MINECART RECIPE

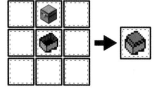

MINECART WITH CHEST RECIPE

2 CREATE JUNCTIONS

To change the direction of your track at junctions, place a lever next to the track. You'll need to be able to reach it from inside a minecart on the track so lay a trail of redstone dust up to the junction and place the lever further away.

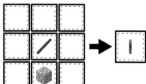

LEVER RECIPE

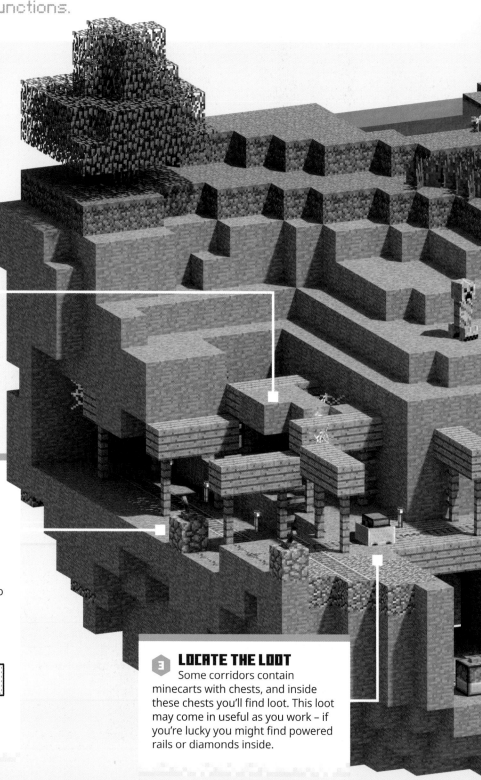

3 LOCATE THE LOOT

Some corridors contain minecarts with chests, and inside these chests you'll find loot. This loot may come in useful as you work – if you're lucky you might find powered rails or diamonds inside.

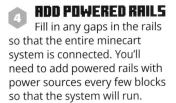

ADD POWERED RAILS

Fill in any gaps in the rails so that the entire minecart system is connected. You'll need to add powered rails with power sources every few blocks so that the system will run.

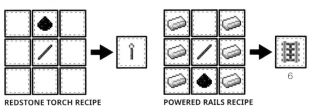

REDSTONE TORCH RECIPE

POWERED RAILS RECIPE

6

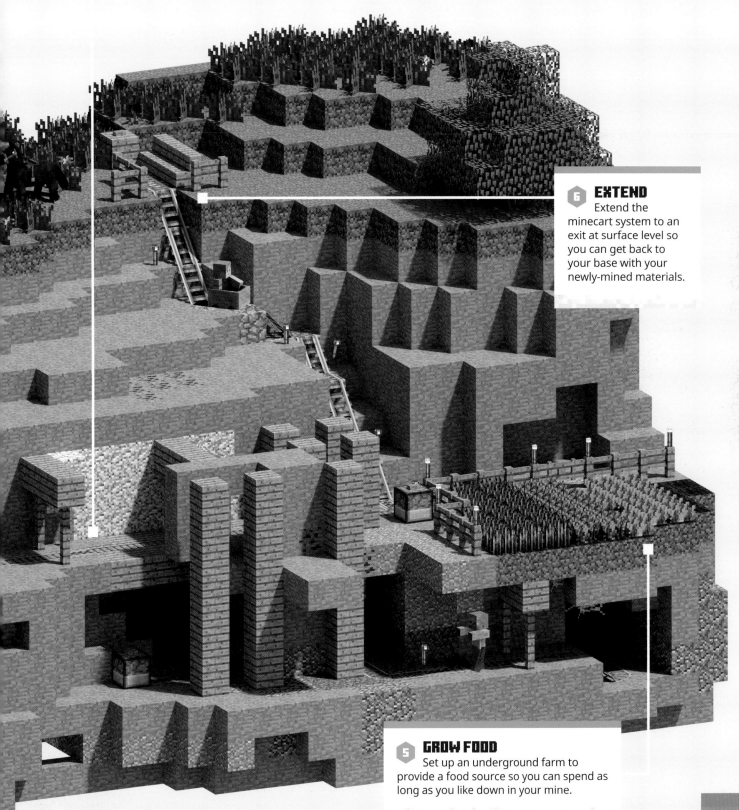

EXTEND

Extend the minecart system to an exit at surface level so you can get back to your base with your newly-mined materials.

GROW FOOD

Set up an underground farm to provide a food source so you can spend as long as you like down in your mine.

MOJANG'S ADVENTURE CHALLENGES

If anyone knows how to have an epic adventure in Minecraft, it's the Mojang team. How many of their adventure challenges are you brave enough to try?

In the spirit of the 404 challenge, spend your first day in a new world collecting resources at surface level. When the sun sets, you have to enter a cave and live below the surface for the rest of the game. This is more interesting if you have a cave that leads to an underground ravine or some mineshafts.

MICHAEL STOYKE
DEVELOPER

We're creating a huge map wall in my Minecraft server. It consists of several maps placed on a wall and zoomed out as much as possible. Together they form a magnificent map showing all the kingdoms of our Minecraft world. I think it's an awesome adventure to create a map wall since you need to explore all the areas that will appear on the map. My challenge to you, great adventurer and voyager, is to create a magnificent map wall in your Minecraft world. Don't bring any beds if you want to make the adventure extra scary and hard.

AGNES LARSSON
DEVELOPER

I call this the Wood Only Nether Challenge: start a new world in Survival mode – the objective is to reach the Nether, but you can only craft things out of wood. You'll need to craft weapons to keep you alive, while venturing out into the world to find the necessary items and materials. You'll have to think carefully before you build and place the actual portal. The challenge can be broken down into six parts:

1 Craft wooden weapons and tools
2 Find some buckets
3 Find water
4 Find lava
5 Build the portal
6 Activate the portal

Good luck!

PATRICK GEUDER
DIRECTOR OF BUSINESS
DEVELOPMENT

With a few friends, try to place sugar canes from the ground all the way to the highest point Minecraft will let you in a 50 x 50 block radius. Use Creative mode so you can fly. When you're done, punch the bottom of each tower of sugar cane and have fun watching hundreds of sugar canes falling from the sky.

MARIANA GRAHAM
ARTIST

31

When the End was expanded to include the outer islands I decided to build a 1000 block long bridge across the Void. This took a lot of time – I walked backwards and placed blocks at my feet. All the while endermen were spawning along the bridge. I made sure to keep my eyes down, but they still caused a lot of trouble simply by trying to push me off the bridge. Why not challenge yourself to try the same thing?

JENS BERGENSTEN
DEVELOPER

I've been playing with the same group of friends on our Survival world for quite some time, and we sometimes like to take time away from building and mining. We've been playing a little minigame where we build a very tall tower of blocks, and place a bed that we all set as our respawn bed. We take turns jumping down (without elytra), trying to place a slime block before hitting the floor. Each time we succeed we build a higher tower, and after 500 attempts we all survived jumping from a 225 block tower!

DANIEL WUSTENHOFF
DEVELOPER

I challenge you to head out on a long journey to discover every biome, and build towns and means of travel as you go. The end goal is to bring back materials to your starter base and enhance it with elements from all over the world. Maybe we are talking about a park to exhibit wildlife and nature, or perhaps biome-inspired buildings. Just use your imagination!

NINNI LANDIN
ARTIST

Why not give Hardcore a try? Set yourself a goal: maybe you'd like to build a fortress in the Nether? Playing in Hardcore mode might not be for everyone but it can be fun for a while and certainly changes your play style. Good luck!

LEONARD GRAM
DEVELOPER

ADD-ONS

Want to customise your Minecraft adventures even further? Some editions support Add-Ons, which allow you to transform the look of your world and change the behaviour of mobs. Let's take a closer look at how Add-Ons work and some of the amazing things you can do with them. You have the power to redefine Minecraft and design your own adventure!

WHAT CAN YOU DO WITH ADD-ONS?

Add-Ons are available for Windows 10 and Pocket Edition, and can be uploaded to your Realm. You'll need to be on the latest version of Minecraft. The first Add-Ons release focuses on mobs. All mobs have three parts: a model (its shape), a texture (how it looks) and a set of behaviours. You can customise all three of these and remix mobs to make crazy new models. You might decide you want a

fifty-foot creeper in sports gear, an exploding pig, a rideable chicken or a baby enderman.

There are two sample Add-Ons available to download from the Minecraft website. Alien Invasion was created by the developers at Mojang for E3 in 2016 and it showcases some seriously cool geometric and textural changes. Check out the modified

iron golem – it's now a hostile alien boss bent on your destruction. And that secret agent villager used to be a skeleton! Castle Siege was made by Sethbling, Blockworks and Mindcrack. You can choose to defend the fort from the attacking mobs, or join the mobs and bring down the fort. Wait a minute, is that villager riding a cow? And is that a giant zombie pigman?

LOOKS AMAZING! HOW DO I GET THE SAMPLE ADD-ONS?

Check out https://minecraft.net/en-us/addons/ to download the sample Add-Ons and read the installation instructions. Once they're installed, open up the world you want to modify and find the Behaviour Pack or Resource Pack tab in the World Settings.

OK, SO WHAT IF I WANT TO CREATE MY OWN?

Great! In that case you'll need to start with Minecraft's unmodified files. Just download the resource packs and behaviour packs from the Minecraft website and get creative.

To change the behaviour of a mob you'll be editing the JSON files. JSON stands for JavaScript Object Notation and it's a script that is easy to understand and edit. You'll need a text edit programme to edit these files, e.g. Notepad ++.

To change the appearance of the mobs you can edit the png files from the resource packs in an image editing tool like Paint or Photoshop and create your own skins.

Add-Ons are still evolving and the plan is to make all editions of Minecraft highly customisable – you'll eventually be able to change the behaviour of blocks. Keep an eye on https://minecraft.net/en-us/addons/ for the latest developments.

NETHER ROLLERCOASTER BUILD CHALLENGE

PART 1

The Nether is a dangerous place, but that doesn't mean you can't have a little fun down there. This Nether rollercoaster is just the thing to lighten the mood and provide maximum thrills.

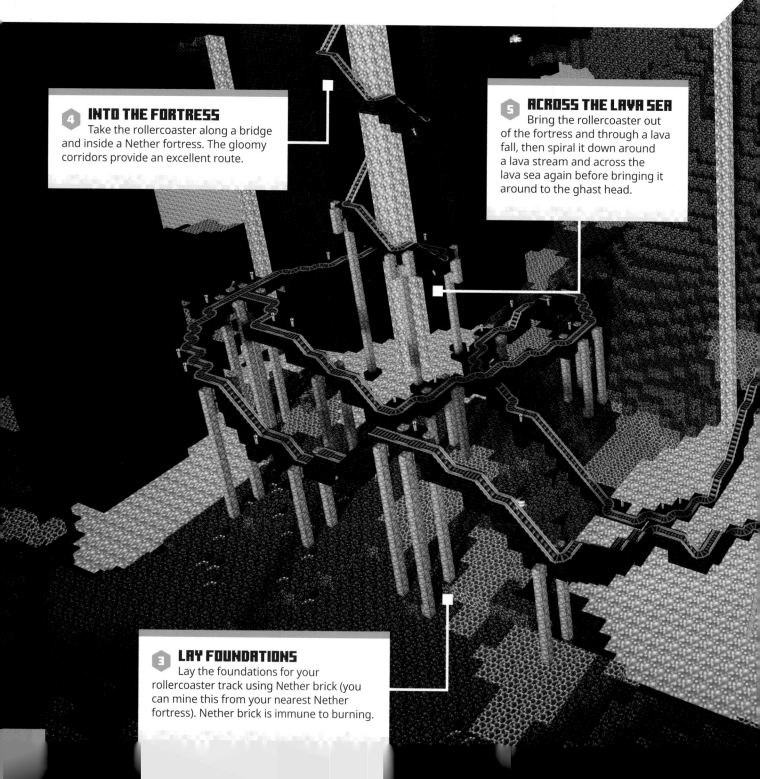

4 INTO THE FORTRESS
Take the rollercoaster along a bridge and inside a Nether fortress. The gloomy corridors provide an excellent route.

5 ACROSS THE LAVA SEA
Bring the rollercoaster out of the fortress and through a lava fall, then spiral it down around a lava stream and across the lava sea again before bringing it around to the ghast head.

3 LAY FOUNDATIONS
Lay the foundations for your rollercoaster track using Nether brick (you can mine this from your nearest Nether fortress). Nether brick is immune to burning.

1 BUILD THE FACE
This Nether rollercoaster starts inside a giant ghast face and emerges from its mouth. Choose a suitable spot to build the face. You'll need to be near a fortress and a sea of lava.

2 ADD A DROP
Add in a terrifying drop that takes the rollercoaster down to a lava sea and then shoots across the surface.

NETHER ROLLERCOASTER BUILD CHALLENGE

PART 2

Let's take a look at the ghast face which appears at the start of the rollercoaster. Use the exploded diagram on the opposite page to help you complete the build.

GHAST HEAD

⏱ 45 MIN ❶❷❸ ◇ MEDIUM

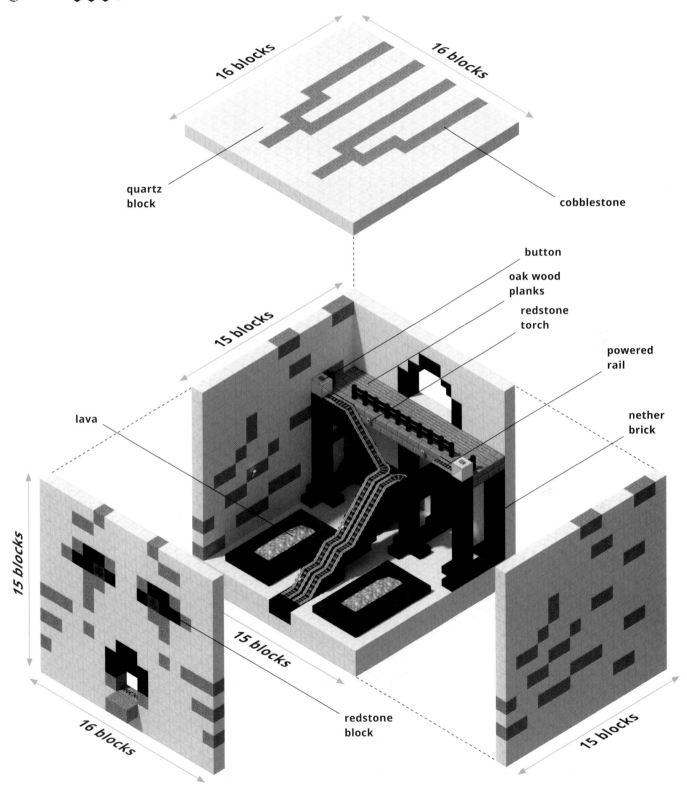

16 blocks

16 blocks

quartz block

cobblestone

15 blocks

button

oak wood planks

redstone torch

powered rail

nether brick

lava

15 blocks

15 blocks

redstone block

16 blocks

15 blocks

WOODLAND MANSION SURVIVAL CHALLENGE

PART 1

Despite their less-than-friendly occupants, woodland mansions are packed with valuable resources. Taking over a mansion will be a challenge, but these steps will help you succeed.

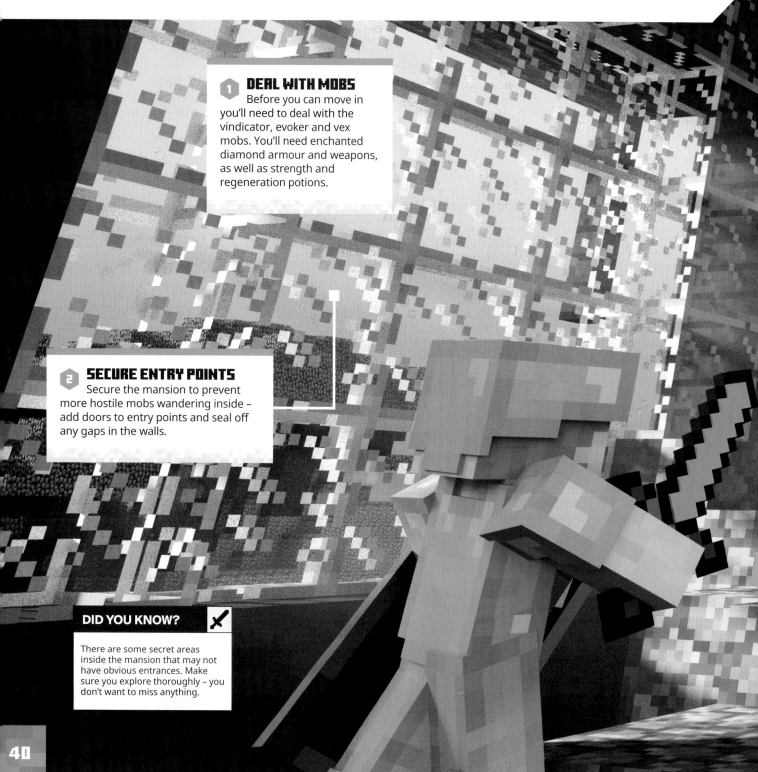

1 DEAL WITH MOBS
Before you can move in you'll need to deal with the vindicator, evoker and vex mobs. You'll need enchanted diamond armour and weapons, as well as strength and regeneration potions.

2 SECURE ENTRY POINTS
Secure the mansion to prevent more hostile mobs wandering inside – add doors to entry points and seal off any gaps in the walls.

DID YOU KNOW? ✗

There are some secret areas inside the mansion that may not have obvious entrances. Make sure you explore thoroughly – you don't want to miss anything.

3 ADD LIGHT
The mansion will be quite dim, so you'll need to light it up to prevent more mobs from spawning inside. Place torches along walls in corridors, and build glowstone chandeliers for large rooms.

4 INSTALL SKYLIGHTS
As well as adding light sources you can also expand the windows to allow more natural light to enter the mansion. The flat roofs are just asking for skylights to be installed ...

WOODLAND MANSION SURVIVAL CHALLENGE

PART 2

Once the mansion is clear of mobs you can begin to import supplies and turn it into a working base.

1 INTERNAL LAYOUT

Choose rooms to use for crafting, smelting, brewing potions and enchanting. There may be a storage room in the mansion containing chests. There may also be a library which can be used as a basis for your enchanting room.

2 WALL

Roofed forest biomes are renowned for being gloomy, which means a higher than usual number of hostile mobs spawn there, sometimes during the day. Add a perimeter wall around the mansion, with an overhang to prevent spiders from climbing over.

3 GARDEN

Once you've built your perimeter wall you can decorate your garden to make it more pleasant. Add lighting to reduce the number of hostile mobs that spawn.

4 PANIC ROOM

Mansions are large structures, and there's a chance hostile mobs could break in or spawn in a deserted corner. In case of emergency build an underground panic room with an escape tunnel leading to a location outside of the mansion. Try hiding the entrance behind a painting and, if you're concerned about creeper explosions, build the panic room out of obsidian.

MINECRAFT TREASURE HUNT

Challenge yourself to an epic treasure hunt in Survival mode. You'll need to find each of the following rare items, without cheating. But first you'll have to work out what the items are by deciphering the cunning clues ...

1 This rare ore can only be found in extreme hills biomes.

2 Catching sight of this ore block among the stone is every miner's ultimate dream.

5 In a hurry? This handy item will instantly transport you to a new destination when thrown. It can be dropped by endermen.

3 For those seeking only the best protection for their horse, you might find this item in naturally generated chests.

4 This object can generate experience orbs but can only be bought from villager clerics.

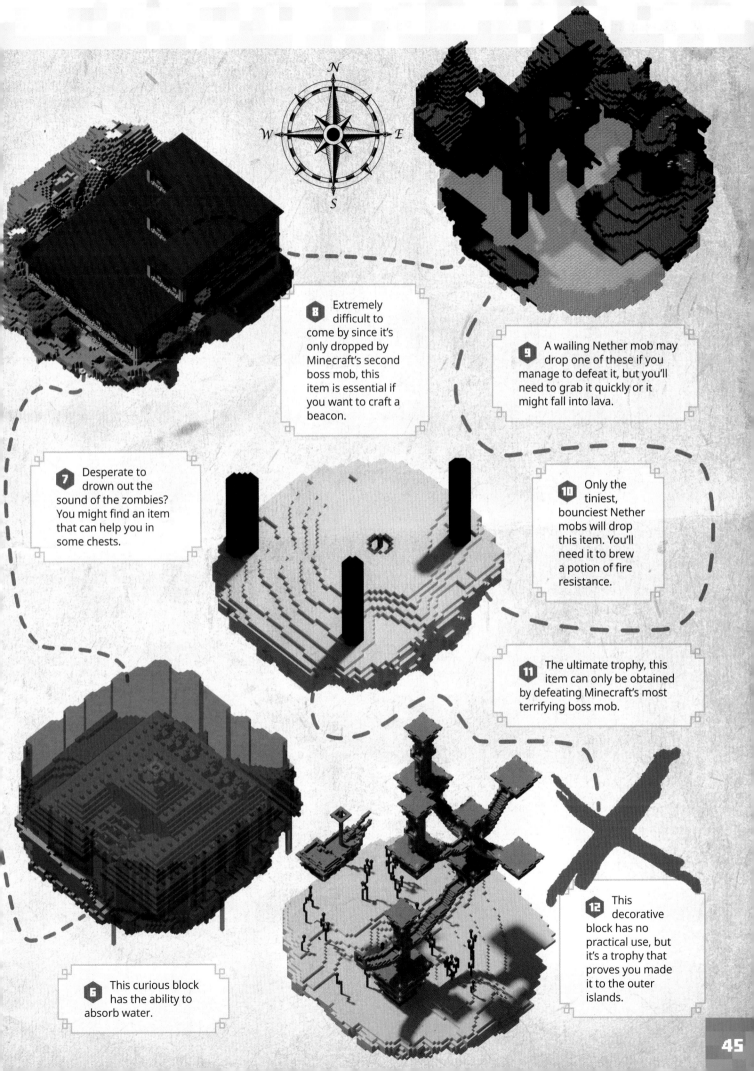

8 Extremely difficult to come by since it's only dropped by Minecraft's second boss mob, this item is essential if you want to craft a beacon.

9 A wailing Nether mob may drop one of these if you manage to defeat it, but you'll need to grab it quickly or it might fall into lava.

7 Desperate to drown out the sound of the zombies? You might find an item that can help you in some chests.

10 Only the tiniest, bounciest Nether mobs will drop this item. You'll need it to brew a potion of fire resistance.

11 The ultimate trophy, this item can only be obtained by defeating Minecraft's most terrifying boss mob.

12 This decorative block has no practical use, but it's a trophy that proves you made it to the outer islands.

6 This curious block has the ability to absorb water.

STORY MODE SEASON ONE RETROSPECTIVE

After eight action-packed episodes, season one of Story Mode has come to an end. Episode six featured several of your favourite YouTubers and they're all missing the game terribly. Here are their favourite Story Mode memories.

SPOILER ALERT! Contains spoilers for Season One

STAMPY CAT

ABOUT STAMPY CAT

Stampy Cat loves to play Minecraft on his Xbox. He's spent over 200 hours in his Lovely World, building, playing games and having fun with his friends. He has added 500 people to his Love Garden, including Mojang and 4J Studios, and he currently has 10 pet dogs that he takes on his adventures with him. Over 7 million people have subscribed to his channel.

My most memorable moment in Story Mode was when I got to interrogate myself. I was lucky enough to be a character in episode six, A Portal to Mystery. In the episode a murder had been committed and Jesse is given the task of determining who the killer is. At this point Jesse interrogates LD Shadowlady, Dan TDM and Stampy Cat. You are able to bring up different evidence and mention pieces of information that one of the other suspects has given to you. At this point Stampy is feeling guilty about something that's not directly related to the murder, which makes him seem like he's guilty. Even though I (of course) recorded the lines I couldn't remember exactly what I was going to say so it was a lot of fun hearing my responses. I accused myself of committing the murder and saw my panicked reaction as I was locked away from the other characters. It was very strange being able to interact with a character I voiced like that, and a really cool moment in the episode.

AMYLEE33

ABOUT AMYLEE33

AmyLee33 plays Minecraft on her PC and make lovely videos for her YouTube channel. Amy loves animals, and her Land of Love is home to 9 dogs and 3 snow golems.

I knew I'd enjoy Story Mode when I realised I'd have a little animal companion, Reuben the Pig! He was super cute! I found myself talking to him like he was my pet dog, trying to keep him safe whilst I researched the endermen at Soren's creepy house. I was more concerned with Reuben than the actual game! When Axel made Reuben the ender dragon outfit it was the cutest thing EVER! I was a very proud Jesse!

When the end of episode 4 drew near and I had to destroy the command block, Reuben, my brave and faithful companion, risked his life to bring me the enchanted sword. Running along the tentacles of the mighty Wither Storm, he delivered the sword to me but then the Wither Storm grabbed him! I literally jumped out of my chair and started smashing the buttons on my controller. "No, no, NO!" I

shouted out loud. But it was no good, I couldn't save him. The game seemed to move in slow motion as Reuben fell to his death. I will never forget those big ol' piggy eyes looking up at me as he fell. I wiped my tears on my cat onesie sleeve, more determined than ever to destroy the Wither Storm. I will never forget the shock of losing Reuben!

LDSHADOWLADY

Recording the voice-over for Story Mode was really fun, especially the recording session with DanTDM. Being in the recording booth together to record the lines made it feel like I was in character and we were actually in the middle of a murder mystery.

One of the cool things about Minecraft Story Mode is that every choice the player makes affects the story. And the way the characters react to what's being said is cool, too.

It was really interesting recording all the line variations for the different situations. I particularly enjoyed recording the voice-over for my character's death scene. I knew

ABOUT LDSHADOWLADY

LDShadowlady began playing Minecraft in 2011 and started her Shadowcraft series in 2013. She is well known for collecting pets, but she doesn't always have the best luck keeping them alive.

there would be a lot of spiders and chaos from reading the script, so I had to be careful when I came to actually play the episode.

I wish I could say that I used my foreknowledge to avoid that gruesome fate, but I led my character right into the trap by accident anyway!

STRONGHOLD SURVIVAL CHALLENGE

PART 1

Challenge yourself to conquer and repurpose your nearest stronghold. Follow these steps to turn it into the ultimate base to prepare for Minecraft's final challenge.

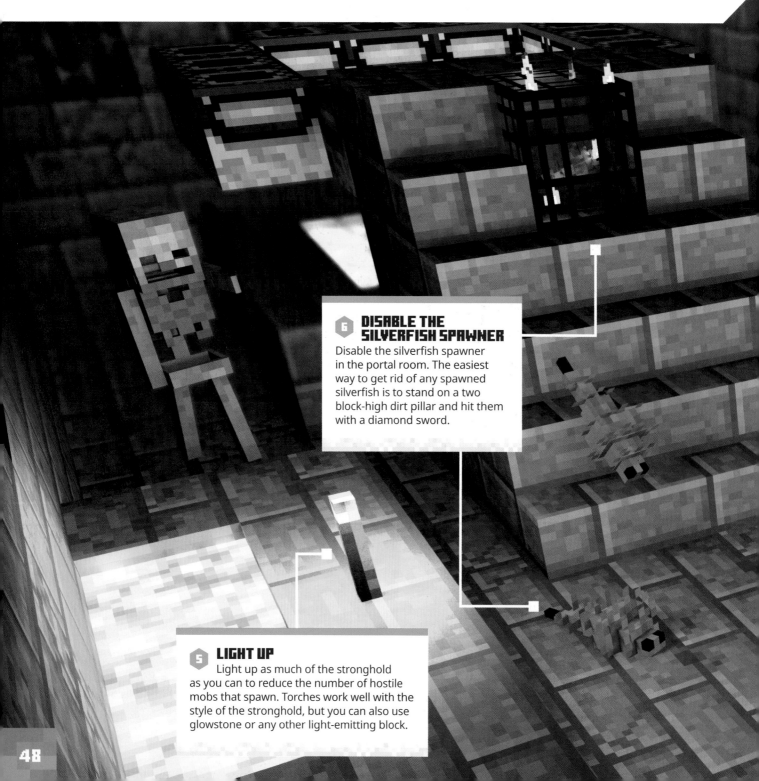

6 DISABLE THE SILVERFISH SPAWNER

Disable the silverfish spawner in the portal room. The easiest way to get rid of any spawned silverfish is to stand on a two block-high dirt pillar and hit them with a diamond sword.

5 LIGHT UP

Light up as much of the stronghold as you can to reduce the number of hostile mobs that spawn. Torches work well with the style of the stronghold, but you can also use glowstone or any other light-emitting block.

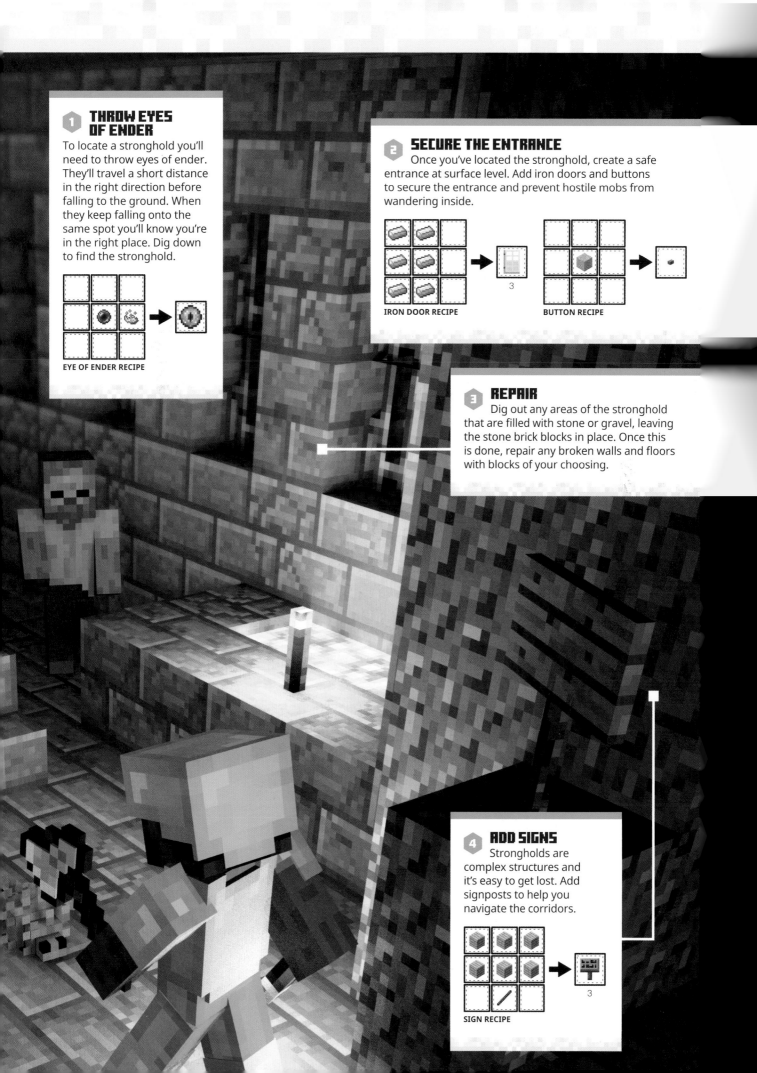

1 THROW EYES OF ENDER

To locate a stronghold you'll need to throw eyes of ender. They'll travel a short distance in the right direction before falling to the ground. When they keep falling onto the same spot you'll know you're in the right place. Dig down to find the stronghold.

EYE OF ENDER RECIPE

2 SECURE THE ENTRANCE

Once you've located the stronghold, create a safe entrance at surface level. Add iron doors and buttons to secure the entrance and prevent hostile mobs from wandering inside.

IRON DOOR RECIPE

BUTTON RECIPE

3 REPAIR

Dig out any areas of the stronghold that are filled with stone or gravel, leaving the stone brick blocks in place. Once this is done, repair any broken walls and floors with blocks of your choosing.

4 ADD SIGNS

Strongholds are complex structures and it's easy to get lost. Add signposts to help you navigate the corridors.

SIGN RECIPE

STRONGHOLD SURVIVAL CHALLENGE

PART 2

Now that the stronghold has been locked down and the hostile mobs removed, you can equip it with the things you'll need to prepare yourself for an adventure in the End dimension.

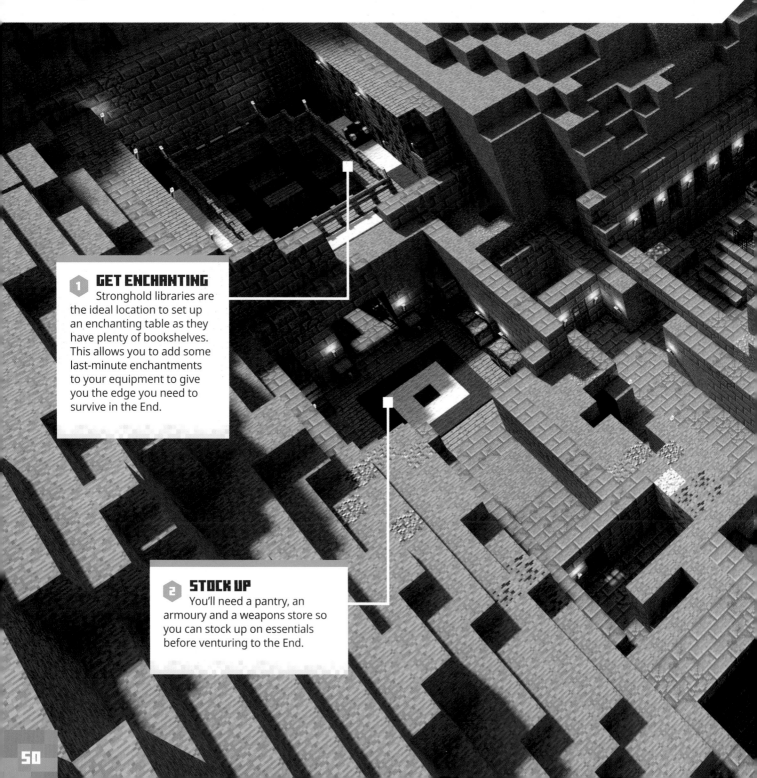

1 GET ENCHANTING
Stronghold libraries are the ideal location to set up an enchanting table as they have plenty of bookshelves. This allows you to add some last-minute enchantments to your equipment to give you the edge you need to survive in the End.

2 STOCK UP
You'll need a pantry, an armoury and a weapons store so you can stock up on essentials before venturing to the End.

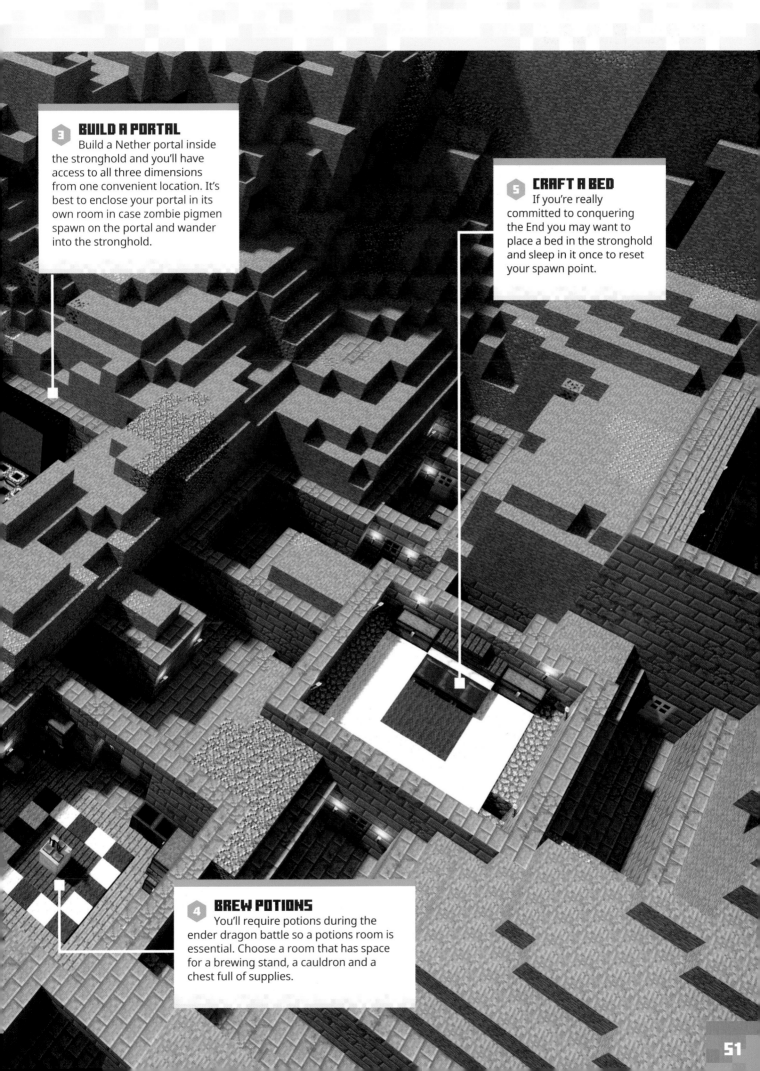

BUILD A PORTAL
3 Build a Nether portal inside the stronghold and you'll have access to all three dimensions from one convenient location. It's best to enclose your portal in its own room in case zombie pigmen spawn on the portal and wander into the stronghold.

CRAFT A BED
5 If you're really committed to conquering the End you may want to place a bed in the stronghold and sleep in it once to reset your spawn point.

BREW POTIONS
4 You'll require potions during the ender dragon battle so a potions room is essential. Choose a room that has space for a brewing stand, a cauldron and a chest full of supplies.

SANTA'S WORKSHOP BUILD CHALLENGE

PART 1

There are no elves in Minecraft, but it's rumoured that the NPC villagers give Santa a helping hand during the festive season. This build is guaranteed to get you in the festive spirit.

1 LOCATION
Spruce trees look very festive, so the best biome in which to build Santa's Workshop is the cold taiga. You could also build it in an ice plains spikes biome for a dramatic backdrop.

2 SANTA'S SLEIGH
Use red blocks and fence blocks to build Santa's sleigh. You can make reindeer out of wood or clay. Don't forget to give one of them a red nose.

6 MINECART RIDE
Create a magical minecart ride around the workshop once it's complete and invite your friends over to visit.

3 WORKSHOP AREA

The villagers need plenty of space to store and wrap all the gifts before they're loaded onto the sleigh. Use wooden blocks for the exterior, with red and green details. Add shelves and storage chests, and use coloured blocks to create wrapped presents. Cover the roof in snow, and add a chimney with spider webs for smoke.

4 TREE

Santa's workshop wouldn't be complete without a tree. Use spruce wood and leaf blocks, and decorate it with coloured blocks and glowstone.

5 SANTA'S CHAIR

Santa needs to put his feet up before Christmas Eve. Build a fireplace from netherrack and an armchair.

SANTA'S WORKSHOP BUILD CHALLENGE

PART 2

Need a little help? This exploded diagram shows you how to get the details right for Santa's sleigh and his reindeer.

SANTA'S SLEIGH

🕐 10 MIN ⬡⬡⬡⬡ EASY

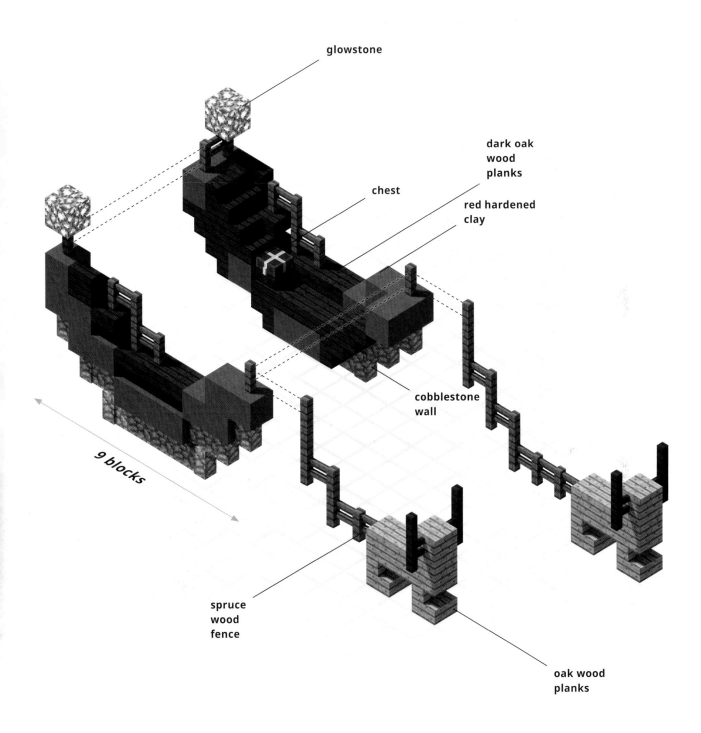

glowstone

dark oak wood planks

chest

red hardened clay

cobblestone wall

9 blocks

spruce wood fence

oak wood planks

Everyone received an enderman-themed bag of loot on arrival.

Parts of the arena were transformed into biomes.

MINECON
CALIFORNIA 2016

MINECON is Minecraft's biggest real-world adventure, and everyone's invited. In 2016 it took place at the Anaheim Convention Center in California. Here are just a few of the epic things that happened at the largest MINECON to-date.

One of the friendly mobs inhabiting the convention center for the weekend.

Twitch provided an incredible 400 computers so visitors could play Minecraft.

Mojang's Vu Bui did a dramatic reading of an excerpt from the first ever Minecraft novel, Minecraft: The Island, written by Max Brooks.

ATTENDEES:
15,000

LOCATION:
ANAHEIM
CONVENTION
CENTER,
CALIFORNIA

CAPE:

MINECON banners were erected outside the convention center.

Visitors practised their archery skills on a lineup of hostile mobs.

Max Brooks talked about why he loves Minecraft, and what inspired him to write Minecraft: The Island.

Things got competitive when 4J Studios challenged a group of YouTubers to a battle.

Visitors who felt like punching a tree could use this simulator to do so.

No MINECON is complete without the traditional costume competition, and the entries were truly inspired.

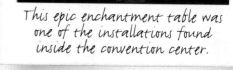

Jeb's panel about the Exploration Update caused excitement, particularly when he announced the addition of llamas.

This epic enchantment table was one of the installations found inside the convention center.

Jeb and Stampy played a dangerous game of 'What's in the box?'

Hypixel created a minigame exclusively for MINECON called Creeper Carts which kept everyone entertained.

Visitors made their mark on this blocky graffiti wall.

Here's YouTuber OMGChad riding one of the prop horses.

EXCLUSIVE INTERVIEW WITH
MAX BROOKS

Max Brooks knows a thing or two about Minecraft adventures, having written an entire novel on the subject. The first official Minecraft fiction, Minecraft: The Island published in July 2017. In this exclusive interview he reveals more about what inspired him to write this epic adventure story.

ABOUT MAX BROOKS

New York Times bestseller Max Brooks is the author of *World War Z* and *The Zombie Survival Guide*. He loves Minecraft and likes to play together with his son, Henry.

What does Minecraft mean to you?
Minecraft is a survival guide for life. It teaches you everything; courage, patience, resilience, all the life lessons you need for making it in the real world. That's why I agreed to write the book. A few years ago, when I first saw my son playing it, I realised 'Hey, this is WAY more than just a game. This is a teacher!' That's when I started playing it myself, that's when I saw how many deep, powerful lessons were embedded in the process of survival. Everything I'd been trying to teach my son, (as well as a few lessons all of us could remember) was right there, and it was fun! The more I played, the more I learned. That's why when I was approached to write a Minecraft book, I jumped at the chance.

'MINECRAFT LETS YOU EXPRESS YOURSELF. IT LETS YOU BE CREATIVE.'

In your opinion, why is Minecraft so popular?
Got me. There's what, 100,000,000 people playing Minecraft all around the world? Who am I to speak for them? Maybe because of the freedom? Maybe because, unlike all those other rigid, level by level, rule by rule video games, Minecraft lets you express yourself. Minecraft lets you be creative.

'I HAD TO LEARN HOW TO SURVIVE. I MADE A LOT OF MISTAKES BUT I LEARNED.'

You seem like a Survival mode/ single player kinda guy. Is that your favourite?

Definitely! Playing on survival gives weight to my accomplishments. Playing on creative is fine, it lets you go farther and faster. But survival, starting with nothing, it makes everything I build, everything I do, so much more powerful because I have to EARN every success. Cut down a tree to get wood to make a crafting table, to craft a hoe to plant some seeds to harvest wheat, to 'bake' bread in the crafting table so I can eat. All those hard, basic steps for the reward of staying alive … so much more satisfying than having everything just handed to you.

Can you tell us about your most memorable Minecraft adventure?

The first time I ever played Minecraft on my own, I started on an island, all alone, and I didn't know how to do anything. I had to learn how to survive. I made a lot of mistakes but I learned from every single one. I don't want to give away too many details, because that experience is the core of my Minecraft novel.

Did you work closely with Mojang on the novel?

Oh yes, we worked as closely as we could given that we're half a world away from each other. The Mojang folks are awesome – they actually care about the quality of their game. That's a rare thing nowadays. So many franchises are just about making money; they don't care what they do or how much they water down their brand. Not Mojang, though. They want Minecraft to stay pure, and real, and true to the ideals of what made Minecraft successful in the first place. They were so helpful in keeping my book within the rules of the game.

'WRITING THE FIRST DRAFT OF ANYTHING IS EASY. THEN THE WORK STARTS.'

What were your sources of literary inspiration for this novel?

Robinson Crusoe. Look no farther than that. My mom first read it to me when I was about eight or nine, and I've been re-reading it ever since. The most amazing part of the book, the part that stayed with me through the writing process of my book, is that Robinson didn't know how to do anything. Daniel Defoe's character wasn't a soldier or an explorer, he was a spoiled, upper-middle class brat who had servants to do everything for him. Being stranded on the island forced him to take care of himself. That's what makes the story a work of pure genius. That's what makes it timeless.

Tell us about your creative process. How did you research the action and the adventure?

The hardest part for me was to keep the book accurate. Even though it's based on my original game adventure, I re-played every scenario in my book. I checked and rechecked to make sure I could do everything I wrote about. I war-gamed every battle. Call it passion or dedication or an obsessive-compulsive mind. (I have all three.)

'MINECRAFT IS A PROCESS. ONE STEP AT A TIME AND YOU CAN DO ANYTHING.'

Did you find any parts of the story difficult to write?

All of it. Writing the first draft of anything is easy. It's all excitement and ego and flow of creative muse. Then the work starts. The following drafts are all about criticism. Is it smart enough? Is it exciting enough? Does everything make sense? Adding and cutting. Rewriting over and over. It's what I

have to do, even when I don't want to. It's a job, no different than any other. Right now, as I answer your questions, I'm halfway through draft three, and there might be more to come.

You're something of an expert in monsters, having written *The Zombie Survival Guide* and *World War Z*. What's your favourite Minecraft monster?
I wouldn't call myself a monster 'expert'. Maybe I just think about them more than most people. I wouldn't say that I had a 'favourite' Minecraft monster, either. Favouritism implies liking something. I hate them all. Zombies never give up, they just keep coming and coming, following you farther than the other mobs, bashing at your door. They never stop! Skeletons can pick you off from a distance. That's really not cool. And if there's more than one

skeleton, they can keep knocking you back before you can get in a couple sword swipes. Spiders just creep me out. Those crimson eyes! You can see them from a mile away. Creepers are just unfair. You're happily going about your business, not bothering anybody and then suddenly you hear that fuse-burning hiss ... if you're lucky you can get away without minor burn wounds. If not ...

What are your must-have inventory items for Survival mode?
For Survival mode all you need to start off is one oak sapling. Plant that and you get an oak tree. Chop down that oak tree and you get apples and wood. You get food and tools and more saplings to plant more oak trees. I've had situations where one oak sapling has made the difference between life and death.

And what's your top survival tip?
Tough question. There are so many. My whole book is a collection of survival tips (not just for Minecraft but for life in general). If I was going to just pick one, I'd say take it in steps. Minecraft, like life, is a process. Don't expect everything to happen all at once. Don't get frustrated or discouraged when things don't work out right away. One step at a time and you can do anything.

If you could ask Jeb to add a new mob to Minecraft, what would it be?
Good question. Maybe snakes? Reptiles are the primary enemy of humans. They're so alien to us because we're mammals. They could be in every biome. Jungles could have multi-block constrictors, deserts could have coiled, one block poisonous rattlers. They could drop items like meat (I've heard snake is pretty tasty), or poison snacks.

MINECRAFT WEBSITE ROUND-UP

The new, improved Minecraft website went live in December 2016 and it's been a huge hit. Helpfully organised into four sections, you can explore the site to find the latest news, merch, insider info and the community's amazing creations.

BLACK SAILS

This animated project was created by JustsomeMonkeys, part of the BlockWorks build team. It's inspired by the piratical TV series by the same name.

CULTURE

The Culture section is dedicated to the amazing community who have made Minecraft the game it is today. This is where the amazing work of people like YouTubers, modders, Add-On creators, server owners, cosplayers and even artists can be found. Projects featured here are inspired by everything from ye olde London town to the spectacle of Chinese New Year.

INSIDER

If you're looking for insider info about Minecraft and Mojang, this is the section for you. The Mojang team post their development secrets, the inspiration behind the latest game updates, downloadable content, game mechanics and loads more. There are frequent 'meet the mob' and 'block of the week' posts, so whatever your interests there's something for you.

BLOCK OF THE WEEK: MELON

Melon was awarded block of the week back in February 2017, due to the fact that it can be eaten and used as a building block. Did you know square melons actually exist in Japan?

MERCH

In this section you'll find the best Minecraft-themed merchandise from around the world. It's not just a bunch of adverts, though – each item has been carefully picked by the Mojang team and they explain exactly why they think it's so special. You'll find everything from posters and books to magnificent mob hats and epic T shirts.

CREEPERSCOPIC VISION
This psychedelic, isometric creeper poster was created by Yanni Davros at J!nx. Yanni has always loved geometry and is inspired by memories of kaleidoscopes from childhood.

CANDY PACK SWEETENS UP POCKET/WIN 10
This sweet texture pack was recently released for Pocket Edition and Windows 10. There are entire floors made of cake and jelly creepers!

NEWS

For the latest game updates and general Minecraft news, look no further than the news section. This is where you'll find the most up-to-date information about all editions of the game, as well as any big news about upcoming products (like the first ever Minecraft novel) or events. You'll also see Tweets from the Mojang team pinned here.

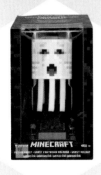

The Minecraft website is also your go-to spot for downloading Minecraft, learning about features like Realms and purchasing the amazing array of merch that's available.

GO TO MINECRAFT.NET AND CHECK IT OUT FOR YOURSELF

PERIODIC TABLE OF MINECRAFT

If you're brave enough to venture deep underground you'll find many of Minecraft's most valuable blocks. From iron to obsidian, most of these blocks were inspired by real-world substances, which is why teachers use Minecraft as a fun educational tool in the classroom. Let's take a look at the real-world inspiration for some of Minecraft's most sought-after substances.

Ob 49

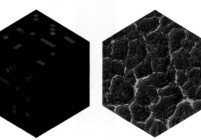

Ma 213

Lv 10

OBSIDIAN

Obsidian is a type of volcanic glass that is produced when lava from a volcano cools rapidly. It's usually black, but can also be brown or green. It's often used to create sharp objects like spears and knives as it tends to break in curves with sharp points. It's used to make jewellery, too. However, it's easily scratched and broken.
In Minecraft, obsidian is also formed when lava cools rapidly – this happens when flowing water hits a lava source block, usually towards the bottom of the world. It's a deep purple colour, but it's the most difficult block to mine due to its high durability, which makes it different to its real-life inspiration.

MAGMA

Magma is molten rock found deep below the Earth's surface. It has a very high temperature.
In Minecraft, you can only find magma in the Nether. It can be mined with any pickaxe and used in traps, since it deals fire damage when touched.

MOJANG STUFF ◉

Check out education.minecraft. net to find out more about Minecraft: Education Edition and how it's used in the classroom.

LAVA

Lava is molten rock that has escaped the Earth's surface, usually through a volcano eruption. When lava cools it can transform into one of several different types of rock.
Minecraft's lava generates all over the Nether, at the bottom of the Overworld, and as surface lava pools in the Overworld. When it comes into contact with water it transforms into various solid blocks. It creates stone if it flows on top of still or running water, cobblestone if it flows horizontally into water and obsidian when water flows into a lava source block. Lava can also be used to make traps as it deals damage when touched.

Pr 16

COAL

Real coal is a combustible black rock that's used as an energy source. It's found in seams within rock and is burned to provide heat or electricity.

Minecraft coal is very similar to real-world coal. Coal ore is found in veins within stone and once mined is burned in a furnace to smelt items. It can also be crafted with sticks to make torches to provide light.

Em 129

EMERALD

Emerald is a green gem found within rocks. It's used to make jewellery.

In Minecraft, you can only find emerald ore in extreme hills biomes, in single blocks. Mine it with an iron or diamond pickaxe and it will drop a single emerald. You can also find emeralds in some naturally-generated chests. Emeralds are used as currency in villager trading.

Fe 15

IRON

Iron is common, and therefore inexpensive. It's used to make steel structures like bridges, to reinforce the frameworks of buildings and to make vehicles.

In Minecraft, iron ore is also common – you can find it from bedrock all the way up to sea level, in veins of 4-10 blocks. It's as versatile as its real-world counterpart, being used to make a variety of tools and equipment.

Ad 56

DIAMOND

Diamond is a solid form of carbon. It's a popular stone for jewellery because it's sparkly and reflects the light. It's also very hard, so it makes excellent tools.

Minecraft diamond also makes excellent tools and weapons due to its high durability. There is no jewellery in Minecraft, yet, but it is also used to craft the most splendid armour in the game.

Au 14

GOLD

Nuggets of gold are found in rocks. Gold is a soft, malleable precious metal that is often used to make jewellery and coins.

In Minecraft, gold can be used to make a variety of items, including tools, weapons and armour. Perhaps as a reflection of real gold's soft, malleable nature, it's the easiest ore to enchant, but isn't very durable.

Li 21

LAPIS LAZULI

Lapis lazuli is a blue semi-precious stone often used in jewellery. It can even be seen on the sarcophagi of the ancient Egyptians.

In Minecraft, lapis lazuli ore can be mined for pieces of lapis lazuli. These pieces are the deep blue of real-life lapis lazuli and can be used as a dye. You also need lapis lazuli for enchanting.

REAL WORLD TREASURE HUNT

There's plenty of opportunity for adventure in Minecraft, but don't forget to look for adventure away from your screen, too. Grab your foam pickaxe, pack some lunch and get your sensible shoes on, then see how many of these Minecrafty items you can find in real life.

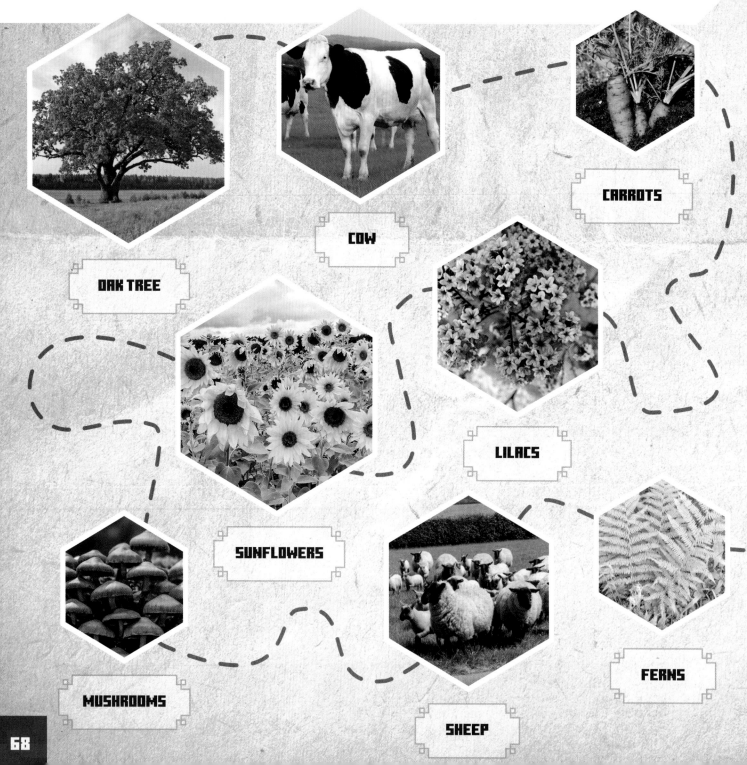

OAK TREE

COW

CARROTS

LILACS

SUNFLOWERS

MUSHROOMS

SHEEP

FERNS

POTATOES

APPLES

BIRCH TREES

WHEAT

PIGS

SPRUCE TREE

COBWEB

SIGNPOST

TULIPS

FEATHER

HAY

HORSE

GOODBYE

That's it for another year! Thanks for reading through the Minecraft Annual 2018 – we hoped you enjoyed every bit of it.

As always, most of the fun packed inside this book could never have happened without you, the players! So give yourself a pat on the back for being awesome.

We look forward to seeing you again next year. In the meantime, happy 'crafting!

Marsh Davies,
Mojang

ANSWERS

PAGE 44-45
MINECRAFT TREASURE HUNT

1 Emerald ore

2 Diamond ore

3 Diamond horse armour

4 Bottle o' Enchanting

5 Ender pearl

6 Sponge

7 Music disc

8 Nether star

9 Ghast tear

10 Magma cream

11 Dragon egg

12 Dragon head